Walking with Spi

Inspired writings by

Melanie Dent

© Melanie Dent 2019

ISBN: 9781096395140

The Seven Principles of Spiritualism

1. The Fatherhood of God

2. The Brotherhood of Man

3. Communion of Spirits and the Ministry of Angela

4. Continuous Existence of the Human Sol

5. Personal Responsibility

6, Compensation and retribution hereafter for all the god and evil deeds done on Earth

7. Eternal Progress open to every Human Soul

To all my Spiritual friends out there.

Be a real serious badass for Spirit. By this I mean don't shy away from speaking or writing your Truth.

Spirit deserves nothing less than you being the best you can be. Let their fire burn within you and don't dilute the Truth.

Don't let anyone douse that fire or try to extinguish your light. Shine all the brighter and let the critics see you fly or run too fast for them to catch.

Spirit Contributors

This book consists of writings inspired by Spirit. Many of them are my own guides so I would like to tell you about the Spirit contributors whose words can be found in these pages

Canaan is my gate-keeper and I actually know little about him other than that he was on the Earth in the 16th century in the Eastern Mediterranean. Canaan and I have already written a book together. He worked as a clerk during his lifetime.

Father Richard Amos was a Roman Catholic priest who passed in 1878 due to Typhus contracted through ministering to parishioners in tenement slums. He is a philosophy guide.

Standing Elk was a Native American Brave of the Lakota tribe. He comes to give me strength to stand for my personal Truth.

David Thomas is the only guide I knew in person. He was my partner for 5 years before passing in September 2008. He has recently come to work with me.

Foreword

I have always had a natural writing ability. When I was a child, I filled countless exercise books, mostly bought with my pocket money, with my own stories. I had an active imagination and was always inventing new stories and characters.

It is only in the last few years, since I made the decision to be a Spiritualist that I have been able to recognise not only where the ability came from but the people who gave me the inspiration.

It's a source of tremendous pride and excitement for me that the words I write come from people who used to walk about the earth living a physical life. I am privileged to have many Spirit guides who are always inspiring me to write down their philosophy for the purpose of inspiring and helping others. That is the purpose of this book.

I know that most words channeled from Spirit into written form come through trance, but I am not a trance medium and have no ambition to be one. I use my intuition and clairaudient ability to get the words that you will read within these pages.

Spirit deserve to be heard

We are all part of the Universal source that many call God. There is a part of God in every last one of us which should be shared and celebrated in every possible way
I am privileged to be able to share this philosophy with you and all I ask is that you share these words with others, either with your friends and family or with a church congregation when you have the privilege of doing a reading in a Spiritualist Divine Service or within a smaller group of friends who meet to connect with Spirit.

Celebrate your own beautiful soul and love the Spirit within you.

Melanie Dent
Reading, United Kingdom
Spring 2019

ACKNOWLEDGMENTS

Thank you to my guides and friends in the Spirit world for their diligent inspiration, without which this book would not exist

Thanks again to my friend Katrina Bowlin-MacKenzie for editing the manuscript.

Thank you to Caroline Lee for the awesome cover design

Thank you to my friend Evey Weinling for sparking my love of philosophy and for being there at a crucial time. Thanks also to Evey's partner Dave Dunford for friendship and support.

Thank you to David Cole and Marion Chilver for encouragement, friendship and the motivation to be the best Ambassador for Spirit that I can possibly be

Thank you to all my friends at Maidenhead Spiritualist church for believing in me.

The darkness many people perceive is in the mind. No place is so dark that the light cannot reach it. Spirit call on us to shine the light into all places, namely hearts and minds. It is a metaphorical darkness that can be penetrated by the light from within us. It is down to us to find the Spiritual light switch and once we are guided to do so we are aware of its location so we can never again be in the dark. Choosing to throw the switch is a step forward to enlightenment. Some find it easier than others, mainly because of self-limitations and the feeling of being undeserving but the great news is that Spirit want us all to be aware of the light that is the closest companion of the love and truth that is our true heritage. We learn of our true heritage through trust in both self and God. Once we have awakened, our perception is heightened and we should never again want to live in the darkness. However, we all make that choice to take the first faltering steps towards Spirit and to enjoy the journey home. The fact is that the keys are all within us already. We just have to be intuitive enough to unlock the door.

Spirit are there to protect us. If we trust in the ability that they have given us then we will be able to find the answer within to almost every situation and question that crosses our physical minds.

Our intuition is the shield against the lies people tell and falsehoods they try to entice us to believe. Intuition is the first line of defence to the integrity of our souls. It must always be trusted above all else. God, of whom we are all part, uses intuition to teach and guide us in all situations and woe betide the physical Spirit who does not, in common parlance, go with their gut. Doing so can save us time and energy.

It may not always be easy to extricate ourselves from people or situations to whom and which we have gone willingly. The fact that we do so is because there is often a lesson that we need to learn from that situation. Trust although the lesson may not always be obvious until we are gifted the hindsight with which to view it objectively. Rest assured that it will be one of the lessons we chose to learn before our decision to be born into our current physical form.

Every lesson we learn is part of the progress of our soul.

A diamond is hewn and created to sparkle. To Spirit we are all rough diamonds but it is up to us to allow them to use the raw material to shape and polish us so that we become a reflection of their light, the spark they place in us can never be extinguished. Life may be hard at times but remember that you came to your current physical form having chosen the lessons and hardships you are to experience for the eternal progress of your soul.

Spirit sent us to earth with beautiful souls and lessons to learn. However physical beauty fades and we make our own appearance, based judgements whether true or not. Spirit see the heart and soul even beneath the metaphorical masks and make up that we may wear and because we are incarnate Spirits, we can conceal nothing from their intense soul penetrating gaze.

We should always strive to see the inner beauty of the soul that most are blind to. The bright light in someone's eyes, the warmth of their smile and the touch of a physical hand, however brief, can mean so much whatever our pathway. A voice raised in anger is ugly, but laughter touches parts of us that make us long for the company of another physical person. We are mirrors of Spirit and we should reflect their light back. As incarnate Spirits we should be our own motivation to be the best person we can be within the restrictions of our physical bodies but our souls are free to seek company and inspiration.

If you must judge others then raise your standards and seek to see their soul, know their pain and comfort them. Outward appearance always belies the true beauty of someone else's soul.

Even when things don't look so good, have faith that Spirit walk beside us every step of the way. They will never let us down

Never let anyone criticise you without giving a valid reason we all have different perceptions of what is acceptable or not. The belief that Spirit stand with you should be your Soul's shield against criticism. Never let anyone tell you that you cannot do something and never let anyone hold you back from achieving your goals. The only thing that stands between you and success is you. Spirit created you and you have that Divine spark within you. Your light will not shine any brighter if you put someone else's out. Always remember that Spirit sees all and knows all. Let this be your motivation to be the best person you can be. Eternal progress of the human soul begins in this very moment

Never doubt that Spirit are waiting for you to ask for help and unlike humans don't see asking for help as a weakness

We are not alone in this world although it often feels like it because the Spiritual path can be lonely. We come from Spirit and they are waiting for us to ask them for help. They will never lie to us or let us down, all they ask is for us to Trust.

Spirit created you to be uniquely you with your own abilities and lessons to learn.

Please don't compromise that uniqueness by conforming to what you think the world wants you to be. Trust your intuition to help you break free of expectation. Be true to yourself and the divine spark within.

Spirit stands with you in the sunlight and walks you through the storm. Never doubt the strength that they give you in knowing the Truth

Spirit knows where you need to be, so having the trust that they will walk beside you every step of your journey is important. If you ask for help, they will give it. But they cannot live your life or make decisions for you. You have to exercise the personal responsibility for your own life and actions, but they are always there to guide and advise so you are never alone.

I DIDN'T WANT TO GO

I never meant to leave
Didn't want you left alone
But the pain got too much
Crushed my life and soul
Tears fall from Spirit
Like a gentle autumn rain
That's where I am now my dearest one
Free from worldly pain

I draw close although
You can't see or hear me now
Know I am there for you every day the same
I feel pride for you, my own flesh and blood.
The fog of grief chokes you
But the light of your love for me never dies

Spirit will guide you through the storm
Be your haven from despair
Just know we are never far
From those we loved.
Some can carry our message
Reignite the hope
And when you come to understand Spirit
love
We will be together again.
Until then, as when I lived
I will always want the best for you.

In theory Christmas is supposed to be a happy time for families to get together, share the love and celebrate, but things are not always as they seem. Spirit urges you to see beneath the surface emotions and not just because Little Jimmy is sulking because he didn't get a new games console. Spirit reminds us that life is about more than material things. There are people out there who may be in an enviable position financially, but they may be lonely and have few friends they can rely on because people only want to know them for their material wealth. The relationships they have may be extremely shallow because of this. Sadly, they are lonely. You can't buy friendship or love, but they buy expensive gifts. However, they may not actually be present and as far as gifts go it truly is the thought that counts. What is the point of buying someone an expensive gift if you are not present to witness their delight?

There are also the homeless people who are on the streets and they have to tough it out alone with no one to celebrate with. They may be estranged from their families due to rifts or addiction or their families have washed their hands of them completely. They may have formed strong bonds with others in the same situation, but still they are alone but for Spirit. At this time of the year humanity does make an effort to include them and try to make life more bearable, but that should continue all year and sadly it doesn't.

Many people dread Christmas as it marks the anniversary or birthday of a loved one who has passed to Spirit. It can be a huge struggle to hold yourself together emotionally and the relief that comes when the guests depart or the kids are in bed must be immense. What they may not realise is that their loved one has been with them every moment, proud of them for holding themselves together and sending healing or even trying to communicate if they sense that someone present may have the ability to see, hear or sense them. Spirit are always present and that is something to be happy about.

Look beneath the surface of the mountains of discarded wrapping paper and see what intuition shows you.

No matter how tough life is you can trust that Spirit will walk with you. They have experienced life in a physical body so understand human frailty and pain. They walk with you through physical pain and medical challenges, celebrate your triumphs and draw close when you shun human company and just want to shut yourself away and cry. Even when you are facing uphill financial strife, a sad reality of life in Britain today, they help you to smile. Smile even when you feel you have nothing to smile about and your smile may help someone feel better about their lot.

Your guides and helpers are always only a thought or whisper away and they are waiting for you to ask them for help. They cannot interfere with your free will but they can advise and guide. Trust in them.

The next two pieces were inspired by my boyfriend David Thomas who passed to Spirit in the early hours of September 23rd 2008.

When someone confides in you give their words due consideration even if you don't agree with their views.

You have no idea what level of emotional strength and courage it took for them to share something so personal. Be mindful of their feelings and don't dismiss them like you would swat a fly. Remember that both kindness and cruelty will come back on you. You have the free will to decide whether you will receive compensation or retribution. Treat everyone the way that you would want to be treated. Their pathway may differ from yours, but they still have feelings because, like you, they are spirit having a human experience.

Note: David would never actually swat flies because he treated all living creatures with respect.

You are not doing yourself any favours by shying away from your personal truth. Speak and stand by it always and tell the truth in love. In this day and age, the Truth is unpalatable for many but for goodness sake be true to yourself and be prepared to walk your path alone if you have to, I did for many years while I was on the earth plain, but I was able to sleep with a clear conscience as a result.

Note David actually said another word while he was giving me this but he knew I would not accept it, it's just the way he would have put it when he was here.

When things are not going as well as we hoped it is easy to blame everyone but ourselves, it is part of the so-called human condition to do so. But we sometimes forget our personal responsibility to be a true reflection of the divine spark of spirit that exists in each of us.

Remember that Spirit loves us and that those who have gone before us have experienced the feelings that we have; the pain, the illness, the anger and self-doubt. That is how they are able to love and guide us, although I am sure they probably shake their heads in despair at times.

Let your light always shine brightly enough to show another the way. Learn to love the broken souls on the fringes of society because they too are Spirit in human form. We often forget that despite our many races, social groups and political beliefs we are the Brotherhood of Man and we all have immortal souls. This is what should unite us but we allow ourselves to view other groups as somehow inferior,

Try to love everyone and treat them with respect

Your Spiritual pathway is as unique as you are. As are the other incarnate souls you meet on your journey. Some come to heal you, others to harm, but you have a lesson to teach as much as you are also here to learn from others.

You have a myriad of experiences to endure in order that you will learn the lessons ordained for you.

The eternal progress of your soul begins as soon as you are born. It is your responsibility to make the most of these experiences as well as being Spirit's light in this often dark and cruel world that you call the earth plane.

Some souls that we meet on our journey are new; others have been here many times and are what we call old souls. The Soul is beautiful although it may become scarred by experience and we are actively encouraged to share our battles in order to help others with the same struggles.

Wear your scars with pride. Trust that Spirit will always hear the quietest plea of your heart. Learn when to let go and move on. We can only do so much to help certain souls but the resources of love and wisdom are infinite due to our being part of the Eternal Divine Spirit.

Some of the souls that we connect with have endured pain beyond our comprehension. But through that pain they have developed resilience and a quiet strength. This is the lessons they have had to learn. You may feel that it is your spiritual duty to try to heal them when in fact they are here to heal you, it may not be easy to discern the difference. But souls are drawn to each other, whether it be for good or bad reasons. The love that you feel for these souls may seem overwhelming and often painful. Send healing and say prayers for these souls but always remember that they have free will.

These apparently broken souls may be a reflection of qualities that you seek within your own self. They may also be a mirror of qualities and ambitions that you have. Respect their experience and trust that they will teach you the lessons you need to learn from them when you are ready. Some only cross your path for a brief time but remember that they had a purpose and try to recall their lesson with fond affection although it may have been painful. Enjoy your journey rather than fixing your eyes on the destination.

SPIRIT WARMTH

Where Spirits are
The air is cold
As would be their touch
Yet spirit hearts are warm
With the love they feel
For those they left behind

Mediums feel and speak
With words that express that love
To physical beings who choose to believe

Love comes through in warm waves
Intense emotions felt and conveyed
Love, resentment, anger and despair
Are emotions that Spirits understand and
share

In the cold winter darkness
Spirit love warms the air
Lights the way
For those living who are lost?
Craving answers from Beyond
Never doubt.
Never fear
The Spirits of those you loved

Are always near

Sometimes when you connect with another physical Spirit you feel sure that you know what your purpose in their life is to be. However, if you are wrong you may still form an emotional attachment to them which, while not necessarily toxic, can nonetheless distract you from finding out what your purpose in each other's lives actually is. Sometimes you may continue to labour under false impressions. Other times Spirit may give you a startling moment of clarity in which you realise that you need to let go of that attachment, which may not be mutual.

This doesn't mean that you have to cut yourself off from them, although if the attachment has become toxic, this may be the best course of action. Release yourself from the attachment and ask for healing for it will be painful especially if you have a true soul mate connection. You need to re-evaluate your experience with this physical Spirit and ask for guidance on how to proceed to the next phase in the relationship if you are certain there is one. Be brave because Spirit gave you that clarity for a reason. They want you to be focused on your purpose and have done this to enable you to take stock. Take time to process what this means for you and be kind to yourself although you are your own worst critic.

The following two passages come through Fr Richard Amos, my philosophy guide who was a Roman Catholic priest while on the earth plain

Never take other physical Spirits you meet at face value or dismiss them as inferior due to lack of privilege or education. Sometimes the simplest souls have the closest connection to Spirit and Mother Earth yet they are often dismissed as being of scant value.

I saw this often in my ministry among the poor and my heart wept for them. They are physical Spirits, same as you are, and so have considerably more worth than society attributes to them. Their humility speaks volumes.

Do what you can to serve your fellow physical spirits as your second principle the Brotherhood of Man suggests. We may be different nationalities, ethnic groups and religions but look at it this way. You wound a Negro or a white man and they both bleed.

I urge you to be humble and to reach out to what your society calls untouchables. Give a kind word or a smile.

If you want to change society then you have to first change the person you see in the mirror

Holding onto past hurts serves you no purpose. In fact, the very act of doing so can tarnish and embitter your soul. It is not always easy to forgive. I was wronged a few times while I lived in your world, but I prayed for and forgave them, it doesn't mean that you have to forget the wrong, but carrying it within your conscious is far from beneficial to the development and progress of your soul.

This works two ways of course; you may have wronged someone even inadvertently but should you become aware of this fact then have the courage to ask that person's forgiveness. If it is not forthcoming then try again intermittently. Don't make it an obsession. A genuine penitent always shows due remorse. Forgiveness brings peace.

You don't know everyone's story. You don't know what struggles they may face daily on waking. By the same token others have no idea of your life.

Try to always be above reproach and reach out in love to your fellow physical Spirits.

We are all God's children and we are also Spirit who has chosen to become incarnate to learn the lessons ordained for the eternal progress of our souls

We are all one with the source of love and healing that is Spirit. We all have the light of Spirit in us so we are all part of the universe. This is decreed by the universal law of Divine oneness.

As such we, in our physical world should view Spirit with reverence and respect. We should give out the love that Spirit places in us although it can be difficult because some people, we rub shoulders with seem only to challenge and test us.

When we work with Spirit, we should treat them with respect regardless of the challenges they may pose. Speak of their love and truth as we endeavour to share their message of love and the fact that our souls are immortal with the Brotherhood of Man.

 I believe that the best way to show reverence is to trust and know that they see the bigger picture and that their knowledge exceeds our limited vision

If we trust and revere Spirit and use their light in us to guide others then that is true reverence

Don't let life get you down. We in Spirit understand the trials and tribulations you face because we endured similar challenges during our time on your earth plain. Try to always meet every person and situation with love although we know that is not always easy. Your loved ones walk with you to ensure that you don't face it alone and if you will but ask, we will show you a way through the storm. Don't give up because you will miss the prize. A physical person's true wealth cannot be measured by money or material possessions. It is shown in the way that you conduct yourself and reach out to others. Remember that you don't know that person's story or any of what they struggle with on a daily, possibly even hourly, basis so treat them as you would wish to be treated. Be true to yourself and stand by your truth. Disappointment will fade and spark in you a genuine desire to do and be better next time. See problems as lessons and opportunities to learn and you will make it.

These words came from Standing Elk during an inspired writing exercise in circle on 18th February 2019

Stand by your personal truth at all times. I realise that it is often difficult in these times where many find the truth unpalatable but speak it anyway. The Great Spirit placed a spark of himself within you. Let yourself be guided by it. Defend what you know to be right and don't let your warrior instinct be swayed by lies and false promises.

I watch you sleep
I see your tears
My hands want to brush them away
Stroke your hair as I often did
Before I left you

I feel your pain
I want you to know
I have not gone away
I am right beside you
You can't see or hear me now
But I hear the unspoken prayers
In your heart
You are still so precious to me
As am I to you
Let physical death not separate us
I walk your path with you unseen

You have a great strength
Of which you are unaware
But I am still here
Be true to yourself
Take your time
One day we will meet again

We are frequently told that we must love ourselves before we can truly love anyone else. However, we must not confuse self-love with ego. Ego dictates and generates a sense of self-importance that is not healthy because, if we are preoccupied with self-importance, people will shy away from us feeling that we love ourselves more than our fellow incarnate Spirits and have no space for agendas other than our own. Be wary
 Be confident in your own abilities by all means but always acknowledge that the ability we value was given to us by the Divine and that we carry a spark of the Divine within us.

Acknowledgement of the Divine according to the Universal law of Divine Oneness is a way to stay grounded and humble. We are all part of the Divine Spirit that many of us call Father God. We need to learn to revere the Divine and let that reverence shine from within us as a light to other souls. Animals too are part of the Divine and they have souls. They cannot speak for their own rights and against those who hunt, kill or abuse them for Profit and personal gain. If you truly value your place in the cycle of eternal life and progress protect and revere animals too.

True reverence to the Divine Spirit embodies love of all life forms.

Be true to the love and light that dwells within you. This isn't always easy, especially when life and experience has jaded you, but know that your loved ones in Spirit continue to love you. They walk beside you every step of your journey. They still want the best for you and will encourage you with the beauty you find in life. Allow your soul to be touched by friendship and love. Find beauty in a flower, a beloved pet, the touch of a friend's hand.

 Open your heart to all possibilities and seek beauty always.

 Remember always that you are a beautiful immortal soul

These words come from Canaan.

My friends, never forget that real true inspiration comes from Spirit
Yes, you may have teachers and role models on the earth plain that you seek to emulate, but don't forget that they are also hindered by a physical body and as such are imperfect.

You are Spirit and come from the divine source. A spark of the Divine exists in all of you. Draw on this fire within when speaking to others. Be guided by your intuition and listen to your guides, helpers and loved ones who have gone before you to walk beside you on your Spiritual journey. They will give you all the inspiration and guidance you seek, but they need you to ask.

Remember that your journey is personal to you and the choices you make before you are born. Others may walk beside you part of the way but they cannot walk your path for you anymore than you are able to walk theirs.

Draw on the Divine spark within, knowing that what Spirit give you is the pure unvarnished truth. Stand by that Truth and look on your origins with reverence.

Even those who do you harm have a part to play in your story.

Through interaction with them you will learn about the person you don't want to become.

Above all be true to yourself at all times, acknowledging God in your life and give thanks for the inspiration He gives.

The celebrated Metaphysical poet John Donne wrote in one of his holy Sonnets Death be not proud. Some have called thee mighty and dreadful but thou art not so.

He was right for physical death is nothing to be feared. It is but a transition home to the Source of love and light whence we came. The source of Divine Oneness of which we are all a part and to which we belong. It is our purpose while living our physical existence on the earth plain to be a true. Reflection of the divine and to stand by the truth which we have come to reveal to those who will listen and look beyond the veil. We should always strive to live in the light and shine it on the darkest areas of human existence. Furthermore, it is also our responsibility to lead the best lives we can as an example of our Divine origins. In that we should try to spread the loving message and reach out to fellow souls whether human, animal or bird. We all have immortal souls and are charged to take care of one another in truth, love and light. Be true to your heritage and vocation and you will succeed in enhancing the progress of your immortal soul

Spirit cannot lie to us, but other physical Spirits can. In these times in which we live the Truth is often unpalatable and we fear ridicule for standing by our Truth and that of God. We should trust our own intuition to discern whether we are being told the truth or not. Our Spirit friends and loved ones give us a truth to stand by and, while it can be difficult at times, it is worth speaking up for. The spark of God in us all reverses truth above most virtues and we should honour it too for in doing so we revere God of whom we are all part. We are part of the Divine source that many call God and are therefore collective energy fragmented into many separate yet complete parts. We call this the Brotherhood of Man. It is our responsibility to shine the light of Spirit into the dark places and be True to the Divine Light of God in us and to speak the Truth of Spirit

These words come from Canaan

My friends consider this for a moment. If someone is given a bottle of 20-year-old single malt whisky is it not, in earthly terms, considered pure sacrilege to dilute before partaking?

So why do many consider it acceptable to dilute the Truth of Spirit with lack of enthusiasm, half-truths and misinterpretation?

The Truth of Spirit, essentially that the soul is immortal is so powerful and you understand this at heart.

The love of Spirit and its light within you comes from the Divine source and myself and my friends in my world often weep for the way in which physical Spirits dilute it in an effort to make it palatable for Mankind.

The truth is often considered to be the enemy but in terms of the eternal progress of your soul it is vital.

Treat it with the respect it deserves

The people with whom you share it may not initially be able to take it in its raw form. So be it. In sharing you are sowing a seed which may germinate and flower in their hearts and souls. If it doesn't then again so be it. You have been true to the Divine in sharing it

The Truth is the lifeblood of Spirit.

These words come from my boyfriend David Thomas

Always be true to yourself. I realise that, in this day and age, this takes courage. There are many who try to sway you from walking your path. Often this is because they are afraid of you and what you stand for. They fear being left behind, yet are not prepared to change their own way of thinking in order to walk part of the way with you.

Be strong enough to love them yet be prepared to stand up for yourself and your own pathway. The progress of your soul is important. You need to be clear on what you stand for. I trusted few people when I was on the earth plain. I was often wary and was able to tell when they had an agenda which didn't include me. I am sure that they often spoke about me behind my back. So what? It wasn't my business whether they liked me or not or even understood me. I don't care for none of that matters to me. It didn't then and it certainly doesn't now that I am in Spirit and can see things more clearly than they likely ever will.

From being true to yourself you will find the inner peace and serenity that is your right as a child of the light.

Those who are afraid to venture beyond the confines of their comfort zone will never learn or progress beyond where they currently stand.

The Divine Spirit, of whom we are all part, gives us everything we will need to face the challenges and learn the lessons allotted to us. It is all inside of us waiting to be discovered. I think that is a pretty amazing truth.

Stand for Spirit and face your fears

Be bold and know that Spirit walks with you as well as dwelling within you. Spirit knows the fears and insecurities we face but dare to be your true self and mind the quality of experience that resides in you. Lessons may be painful but he who fears to take a leap of faith will be known for lack of accomplishment rather than the great potential they have. Spirit gave you everything you needed to lead a rich and full earthly life. Draw on that at every turn and invoke their help. The tag line of the famous movie The Shawshank Redemption says fear will hold you prisoner but hope will set you free.

Have faith and hope. Trust in your higher self. Do one thing each day that terrifies you and, little by little, your eternal soul will progress

Always fall in love with a soul rather than a face. Physical beauty deteriorates with the passage of time but a soul is always beautiful. Even souls tainted and marred by experience have their beauty and are immortal and indestructible. Lust waxes and wanes with the moon and can foster bitterness and resentment. Base all your human relationships on the soul within and nurture connection for the sake of the brotherhood of Man and your own eternal progress. A true soul connection survives physical death and the soul that has passed will remain forever with you to guide, strengthen and sustain you through life's hardships and trials. A true soul connection with another physical Spirit will enrich your life beyond measure.

These words were inspired by Standing Elk

Mother Earth is life sustaining but generations of physical people have raped and plundered her for her natural resources. The water she holds sustains life and the rocks and caves in her surface provide sanctuary from evil and foes.

My people always respected the earth, as do other native tribes throughout the earth. They have so much to teach us. Our reward has often been marginalisation, isolation and genocide. Our people spilled our own blood and the blood of other nations in Mother Earth's defence and that of our traditions and way of life.

When will it be accepted that we do not own the Earth. She is a gift from the Holy Great Spirit and it saddens us deeply to see how she has been pillaged and abused in the name of so-called material progress which is not in line with the progress of the soul

I urge you my friends to protect Mother Earth. Accept her for the life she gives despite being broken. All the material wealth you may seek or possess is nothing in the sight of the Great Spirit. Remember that always.

Don't look elsewhere for the answers

 The Spirit within you holds the key to the universe. The answer lies within you.

So often we get caught up looking for answers to the pertinent questions in life.

However, as Spirit in human form, we come to earth already equipped with the knowledge and ability to find these answers within ourselves. We need to learn to trust our intuition, which some believe to be the GPS of our souls in modern parlance. We need to learn and search inside ourselves for the answers that we seek.

How can we sing the Lords song in a strange land?

Well as we are Spirit who chose to be born into a physical body, we are in a strange land that is not the world of Spirit whence we came.

Spirit needs us to sing their song, spread their beautiful message of love and the immortality of the soul. They have given us everything we need to cope with the lessons, challenges and hardships that we are here to learn. It may not always be easy but nothing worth doing ever is. We need to be prepared to stand up for Spirit and fly their flag without backing down and surrendering to lies and falsehoods. On our way we need to be true to ourselves and the Spirit within us. Reach out to your fellow physical Spirits in love and truth. It may well be thrown back in our faces and rejected. It matters not.

Hardships enable us to be the best we can be, although it may sometimes be hard to find the lesson. Those we meet along the way fill our journey with colour.

Some bring pain, others joy and love but everything that happens does so because we made choices before we came here.

Make a choice today to stand up for Spirit and trust their guidance and that of your higher soul and intuition

In all things show reverence to the divine. The eternal progress of your soul begins the moment you choose to progress and stand by the truth of Spirit. Let them and your higher self be a bright light that others can be guided by. Above all live your life for love.

When you come to Earth you become aware of the passage of time. However, you have no idea of how much has been allotted to you or what your purpose is to be. Your origins from the World of Spirit are forgotten as well as the lessons you chose to learn.

Therefore, it is sensible to make the most of every moment. Treat each day as if you know it is to be your last. Learn to embrace lessons as experience and do your utmost to do right by those whose pathways you cross. They may well not treat you well, but you have no idea of what they may have to struggle with so do your utmost to always show compassion and kindness without prejudice or judgement. In short, treat them as you would wish to be treated and always be aware of your heritage. As soon as your soul awakens take every opportunity to learn more and connect with the Source whether you call it God or the gracious Spirit it matters not. Embrace life's lessons and see the beauty in every soul whether human, or animal. Above all do not place emphasis on material wealth. The true wealth of a physical Spirit lies in the way they connect with God and the world in which they live, not in how much money they have for they cannot take it back Home with you. A man's true wealth is found in his heart and soul.

The light of the Divine is within you

Revere it and use it to be a light on someone else's pathway and never be too proud to ask others for help.

We are here to teach one another.

Remember always that your soul is immortal. It survives physical death. Do not allow life to tarnish it too much. Strive always towards its eternal progress. Try to always see the light and beauty in the souls of other physical Spirits and nurture them with love. However always allow others to make their own decisions and use their free will to good effect.

Intuition

You meet someone
Somehow you know
If their intentions are for good or ill
 God speaks to you
Letting you know
Use your free will wisely

Situation may seem dire
Lacking thought maybe on your part
But here you are
Trust and listen
The true path should be clear
Intuition is a light
On the darkest of paths
Use it

Courage is something that we all possess. As with many attributes that God has placed within us. However, we may not be able to recognise it. Some of us may spend our physical world looking for something which was there from our birth. We may not be called upon to use it, but that doesn't make it any less real.

In the story of The Wizard of Oz the wizard could be viewed as a wise teacher. He sent Dorothy and her friends on a dangerous quest to get the Wicked Witch of the West's broomstick in return for what they craved. However, he knew that they already possessed these things within themselves.

We all possess what we really need to tackle the challenges of the life we have chosen to experience. It is a matter of looking within. We cannot find these things outside but for some it takes many years to realise this.

Courage is the ability to act in spite of fear, of rising above that fear and daring to look it in the eye. When we do this fear ceases to have power over us. If only we were told this in our Mother's womb? But if we were born with every advantage, and I am not speaking here of financial or material advantage or breeding, then life would be an empty pathway along which we would tread without learning or being able to advance the progress of our souls. We come here to learn lessons accompanied by God within us and our Spirit teams. We also have our soul family who we learn to recognise due to previously shared bonds of experience. No one is truly alone in this physical life if they value Spirit and their essential heritage. Don't let fear be your prison. See it as a temporary setback and a challenge to be overcome. Allow yourself to step outside your comfort zone and expand your boundaries. This will help you to break free of convention and your self-limiting beliefs. There are many who fear your advancement so they try to hold you back. The best way to deal with that is for you to let them see you soar way above the limitations they place on you as well as those you place on yourself. Be like the Eagle, soar wild and free and allow your light to be a beacon to your fellow physical Spirits.

Gone from our sight
But never our hearts
Spirit walk with us every step of our way
We feel their love
Their strength fortifies us
Through good times and bad
We hear their words of wisdom
All of our days on earth

For me one of the most amazing things
about Spirit is that those we love never truly
leave us.

We may have an ability to connect with our
loved ones or we may not but we know that
their love for us never dies. Too many still
believe that physical death is the end but we
know it is only the beginning. The human
soul exists long after the demise of the
restrictive physical body. It exists to comfort,
advise and encourage us on our way.

The loss can be an emotional devastation, but we always have a choice. We can allow ourselves to be held ransom to grief or we can embrace the freedom that we gain. The freedom to explore and understand our own souls and to choose a new pathway. Indeed, the passing of a loved one often causes us to seek a new truth within ourselves and that can be incredibly liberating.

Our loved ones in Spirit want us to move on. They want us to carry on with this physical life. They want us to celebrate our uniqueness and discover our own connection to, and relationship, with the Divine source of oneness which exists in every last one of us. They want us to be inspired and to be true to our divine origins. Doing so can be a source of peace and joy.

These words come from David Thomas

If I were you, I would never underestimate anyone or anything
 Things and people who appear the most fragile often have the greatest strength.

Take the butterfly. A beautiful creature from the humble origins of a lowly caterpillar. To break free from the cocoon of development and transformation it beats its wings many thousands of times to break free and begin the next phase of its life on earth.

So too are we like the emerging moth or butterfly. We beat our seemingly fragile wings against the cocoon of life experience that shapes and moulds us so that we can be the best Spirit need us to be
 Those of you who knew me when I was in my physical body will know that I had a great admiration and respect for butterflies and hated to see them hurt or damaged.

Butterflies and moths are a widely recognised symbol of the presence of Spirit and I know that many of you believe this.

Don't let life crush you. Your wings are a lot stronger than you think. Celebrate your delicate strength and recognise where it came from.

These words come from Fr Richard Amos. Due to the references to Jesus I recommend that this reading be used only in Christian Spiritualist church services.

My child, never accede to the belief that compassion is weakness.

Those who exhibit compassion are often underestimated and misused by those who don't recognise the strength of compassion. Don't buy into this for compassion is strength and a huge building block in the progress of your soul. Our Lord the Nazarene, was known for his compassion and understanding. Even in the painful act of the physical death he chose to endure he reached out in compassion to those crucified alongside him.

When I served God on the earth plane, I was often moved by the compassion that I saw from my fellow men and the strength that they showed despite poor circumstances. I was constantly reminded that the rich and powerful, who had the material means to bestow the greatest compassion and benevolence often chose not to for they feared that kindness would result in exploitation by the poor. However, it was rare that I actually saw this to be proved true. To me it was often the poorest and most downtrodden who excelled in compassion and gave often beyond their means to help others. I tried to help others as far as I could by exhibiting a Christ like compassion and often the largest contributions to the mission, I served came from those barely able to feed and clothe themselves or their families. Let these people be your example of love and humility and beware those who trumpet their material wealth yet don't employ it to be humane. Thank those who give of limited means and remember that there is always someone worse off than yourself.

Those who are poor in means are often far richer in Spirit.

These words come from Canaan.

My friends, don't let your ego get a foothold. Celebrate your own victories and achievements by all means. However always remember to acknowledge God as the source of it as all that you are comes from him and is within all of you.

Those who celebrate themselves without an acknowledgement of God or whatever name you give to the ultimate power will soon fall afoul of their own ways. Always remember to exhibit humility and grace at all times and don't be afraid to ask for help. Spirit are always ready to help you but they are not able to without your consent because they cannot override your free will.

Always be deserving of Spirit's help and acknowledge them in all ways whether verbally or in the unspoken pleas of your heart and soul. Do not serve Spirit for personal gain. Look within yourself and see that you are there to serve Spirit and your fellow physical Spirits.

Those who serve Spirit for material gain and praise will soon fall spent by the wayside as they have not called upon the divine source of their power and have neglected to realise that they cannot pour from an empty cup. In the same way those of you who work tirelessly for Spirit and their fellow men need to learn to receive as well as to give for giving alone will soon deplete your energies and weaken them although you serve with a pure heart and true dedication.

Always acknowledge God with reverence and give thanks for the blessings he gives you.

Life's storms
Buffet the soul
Deplete and drain the will.
But strong hearts and souls
are always aware that Dawn will come
And that the sun will rise again
Those who have Spirit in their mind
The true heritage
Stand strong
Speak your truth and know
This storm is but a step
On the narrow and uneven path
Back Home

These words come from Canaan.

My friends, never apologise for being true to yourself or standing by the Truth of Spirit. Many in these modern times find the truth unpalatable and therefore shrink from it. Those who do have not yet experienced the awakening of their souls. Do not judge for you were once like them.

You need to pray for awakening of souls so that more can become aware of their true heritage, that they are Spirit in physical form.

Reach out in love and encouragement. No one is beyond redemption although to you, with the inability to see the whole picture, it may seem so.

Those who appear irredeemably wicked are also physical Spirits who have simply chosen a different pathway to learn different lessons. It doesn't make their pathway wrong. They just have a different concept of personal responsibility. War Lords, criminals and corrupt politicians will eventually be brought to account for the atrocities they have committed and their retribution will be fitting. It may seem that they are getting away with it, but my friends in my world and I see everything and know what is in their hearts and minds in every passing moment. They cannot escape from the hand of Divine justice but it is not your place to try and bring about their downfall. I urge you to leave this to Spirit although I realise that this may be difficult for those of you who have been wronged.

Just keep being the light of Spirit and do not allow those in ignorance to dim your light. Shine even brighter and wield the sword of truth in all your dealings with your fellow men and women. Then you will know peace and be able to sleep comfortably knowing that you acted according to your own integrity.

The soul is like an iceberg. I do not mean that it is cold and unfeeling, quite the opposite in fact. The majority of the ice berg is submerged below water. As is the case with the soul. So much is unseen by other physical Spirits but it is there. Its depth is indestructible. Someone in your soul family will be able to see and discern some aspects of your soul depth, but not all. Try at all times to be encouraged by the knowledge that you are part of God and be true to the blessed gifts and insight with which He has gifted you. Be a light to your fellow men and always Trust that God, the Great Spirit or whatever you may call him knows what is best for you.

These words come from Standing Elk

The Great Spirit has placed a spark of himself within all of you. This spark is designed to be fanned into a fire of passion and action.

 The resulting fire can be used as motivation to speak against injustice and to share the Great Spirit's teachings with like-minded souls.

Throughout the ages my people have been victimised and subject to great injustice and ignorance of our ways. In all your cowboy movies my people are seen as the villains simply for defending our culture and ways of life. So too are Spiritual people misunderstood for their purity and higher awareness of the ways of the Spirit World and how to be within that world yet apart from it. Be a light to your fellow men and be discerning in your trust. Many have agendas disguised as good intentions but which are, in fact, anything but.

Once a year my people hold a fire ceremony in which we acknowledge the clearing out of the mind and physical life of people and feelings which no longer serve. It is a cleansing of the soul and a good thing to do. Hold your own fire ceremonies and you will succeed in moving past that which holds you back and embracing what will move you forward. In your world this may mean cutting toxic people from your life, distancing yourself from them and situations which do not benefit the progress of your soul. Always be prepared to move if needs be. I don't necessarily mean moving from the geographical location where you reside as this can be disruptive and costly in material terms. I mean simply find new friends and places where your soul can progress and teachers who don't hold you back for selfish reasons. Let intuition be your guide and best friend in all matters.

Above all allow the fire to burn within so that the flames of desire to serve the Great Spirit will spark the same passion in others. This is the destiny that the Great Spirit wants for you.

Gracious Spirit come
Light the fire within
Open our minds to your ways
Stir our intuition to trust you
And prove our worth
In this strange land
to which we chose to come
Grant us endurance
Serenity to accept
And wisdom to know
That you are always with us.
Heal those wounded in mind and body
With your loving touch
Spark love in all of us
For our fellow men
Give us the strength to stand by your truth
No matter what it costs
And free us from the prison of insecurity
and fear
Enable us to stand
Even if we stand alone
For you stand by us all.
I ask all this in love, light and Truth and
always in your name
Amen

Author note. This reading has aa special meaning for me as I read it during my first platform experience on 28th April 2019 when I did a service with David Cole.

My friends, many of you give a lot in service to God. You give your love, time and material resources and that is commendable. Yet, in doing so, you often forget yourself. It is not selfish to ask for healing or help when you need it, nor is it a weakness to ask for such things. Service can deplete your physical and emotional resources.

Healing comes from God, of whom you are a part. Your soul undergoes strain from the emotional part of the lessons you came here to learn and you can't pour from an empty cup.

Truly Spiritual people, with whom you may have a strong soul connection, may intuitively have recognised the pain within you. However they cannot help you heal if you are not prepared to admit to the pain within. Kind words and a gentle touch of the hand can bring healing.

But true emotional healing is not possible unless you are prepared to lay bare your soul. Many of you feel pain from past hurts, some of which a physical Spirit with a true soul connection to you may be able to discern in part. You feel that you survived so the pain is best left there, but experience may teach different. If you aren't able or prepared to own and deal with that pain then God may bring healing about in unexpected ways which may force confrontation or loss of control. Don't be afraid to be emotionally vulnerable because the right souls can bring you healing with love. Tears are not a weakness.

Trust always for true faith and trust in God brings its own rewards.

Final words

Gracious Divine Spirit

Thank you for allowing me to share your inspirational words. I thank you for the fact that my guides helpers and loved ones are always close to me and that I am able to be aware of their presence. I thank you also for working with me to bring this book into existence and I pray that it will bring comfort and inspiration to many.

I ask that you send healing energy to all those at this time according to their need, whether they be human or animal as we all have immortal souls.

I ask that you be with our government and world leaders as they work towards peace and the resolution of issues which affect them and those they govern at this time. I ask that you be present in places of conflict and inspire them to work towards peace and the laying down of arms.

I ask also that you be with all people who are imprisoned at this time, no matter what they may have done. Help us all not to be judgmental and inspire them to understand the errors of their own ways and those of whoever has placed them in their current situation. Please grant them understanding.

I ask all these things in love, light and Truth in your name.

Amen

Thank you for reading Walking with Spirit. I ask that you leave a review on the website where you purchased this book so that others may find it.

By the same author

From Canaan with love:
Messages from my guide

While the inspired messages of many
celebrated Spirit Guides such as Silver
Birch are available in print others are not.

For the first time in this volume the words
of a guide named Canaan have been
collected with the aim of spreading the
central message of Spiritualism.

The human soul is eternal and
indestructible. The love of Spirit should
be shared with mankind

In this collection of inspired writings
alongside the interpretation of Canaan's
channel may you find peace, strength a

21051370R00050

Printed in Great Britain
by Amazon